IT COULD HAPPEN
TO YOU

IT COULD HAPPEN TO YOU

A Testimony of Overcoming a Chronic Illness

Evangelist Georgette Mayberry

It Could Happen to You
Copyright © 2012 by Evangelist Georgette Mayberry. All rights reserved.
Reprinted 2018.

No part of this publication may be reproduced, stored in a retrieval system or transmitted in any way by any means, electronic, mechanical, photocopy, recording or otherwise without the prior permission of the author except as provided by USA copyright law.

Except otherwise stated, all scripture is taken from the *King James Version* of the Holy Bible (Public Domain)

Cover Photo Credit: Ricky Jr.
Owner and Photographer of
Flemings Photography

Published in the United States of America

ISBN: 978-1-949362-56-5 (*sc*)
       978-1-949362-55-8 (*e*)

Library of Congress Control Number: 2018953009

Published by Stonewall Press
4800 Hampden Lane, Suite 200, Bethesda, MD 20814 USA
1.888.334.0980 | www.stonewallpress.com

I dedicate this book to my grandmother, Virgie Harrison (deceased). Grandma, you are truly missed and I love you.

Grandma, what a great inspiration you were. A woman of God who did your duties unto the Lord. You passed the tests and trials. You fought the good fight of faith (2 Tim. 4: 7).

No matter how hard, rough, and tough it was for you, you made it through. You made it to heaven's best. Our father, which is in heaven, called you home to a place where you are safe now. God dried your eyes permanently as he loved you unconditionally.

See you later, Grandma. You're at peace. You're home now.

Love,
Your granddaughter—Gee

Do you know about the **POWER** of **GOD**?
Is **FLESH** standing in **YOUR** way?
Who do you serve, **GOD** or Satan?

Contents

Acknowledgments 11
Introduction 13

Chapter 1	I Woke Up One Morning 15
Chapter 2	My Appointment 21
Chapter 3	Test Results 25
Chapter 4	Multiple Sclerosis 29
Chapter 5	Having a Relapse 33
Chapter 6	A Call from My Physician 37
Chapter 7	Walk by Faith, Not by Sight 41
Chapter 8	Changing My Mindset 43
Chapter 9	It Could Happen to You 45
Chapter 10	A Heart Filled with Compassion 47
Chapter 11	The New Me 49
Chapter 12	Covered by the Blood of Jesus Christ 51
Chapter 13	My Friend Had a Dream 55
Chapter 14	Know That You're Blessed 57

Chapter 15	Persevere	59
Chapter 16	One Year Later	63
Chapter 17	What Is Multiple Sclerosis?	69
Chapter 18	How to Eat	73

Words of Encouragement 75

Acknowledgments

WITH ALL OF MY heart I want to thank my Father, my Friend, my Lord and Savior Jesus Christ. I acknowledge none of this would be possible without you. I acknowledge that you are the provider of my life. You taught me that there is no difficulty in life that comes my way that you can't cause me to triumph in and over. I love you, Jesus!

To my daughter, Antwanette, who has been with me from the beginning, I'd like to thank you for all your support and hard work in a time when no one else was there. As your mom I want to say, "I appreciate and love you with all my heart. You mean the world to me."

To Sister Brigitte Coston, thank you for allowing God to use you to take such beautiful photographs that I was able to use them for this book. Thank you for all your support as well as all that you have done for me.

To my cousin, Evangelist Channie Linton, thank you for encouraging me through it all. When I felt like giving up, you coached me through the difficult times of my life, and for that I appreciate you and love you.

To my Sisters in Christ, Daughter of Zion Shulawn and Daughter of Zion Charity Jones, from Sacramento, CA. I thank you for taking time out of your busy schedules to come and help me. I am very grateful to you both. God bless you.

Introduction

THE TRIALS OF LIFE can make you feel as if you're lifeless. Yet at my weakest state I found strength and newness of life from above to deliver me out of my brokenness. The unexpected happened to me on August 5, 2010.

I felt so afraid and I truly thought my life had come to its end. Can you imagine being fine and normal one day and all of a sudden, when you least expected it your life took a drastic change? If everything went from normal to abnormal what would you do? One minute I was walking fine and next thing I know when I woke up I was numb from neck down to my foot on my right side. What could I do? My faith stood before me as a question mark or as a mocking of the devil's voice. Can you trust in your God now? My inner soul waited for my answer…would I trust in Jesus or the report of man? Are we prepared to handle a raging storm in the form of a trial? Ask yourself the question, if God were to take you on a journey and suddenly something happened to you that hindered you from providing for your family; would you be able to believe that God would be with you and guide you safely through your storm? Could you deal with the negative reactions of people because you have changed but they don't understand what's going on with you? Could you walk by faith, or falter because in your present dilemma it's difficult to see his unconditional love before you? Could you inhale his breath of life when you're feeling lifeless? Are fear and doubt trying to befriend you? Do you find yourself pondering on the question, "Can you stand the test?"

My experience has allowed me to grow closer to Jesus. I learned Jesus is my all. In my greatest battles I learned that it doesn't take a great army of men to fight with me; Jesus is all I need and the battle is already won! This trial has taught me to hold onto him in every situation. Jesus showed me how to put him first. No matter how much pain I endured, Jesus said, "I will never leave you nor forsake you." He said, "I am the truth, the way, and the life." He said, "I give you peace," even when it was hard for me to trust him. Jesus said if you don't suffer with me you won't reign with me. I pray that my suffering is reigning in such a way that God will be glorified through this book. I pray that what I suffered is helping, strengthening and encouraging you to reign over whatever dilemma you may be confronted with.

Chapter 1

I Woke Up One Morning

On August 5, 2010, a bright sunny morning, I got up from my bed to get ready for work. I felt something wasn't normal. I was numb on my right side from my neck down to my feet, and I thought, *Wow, this is different*. My left side was fine, except for a little numbness in the fingertips of my left hand. I didn't worry about that, not as much as my right side. I couldn't use my right hand at all. My right leg was dragging and felt very heavy. I couldn't keep my balance. Fear was in my heart, but I kept it to myself. I struggled to take a shower and put my clothes on. It was difficult to button my shirt. I put on a pullover shirt instead, and could barely do that.

I went to work anyway. I was certain that this was the calm just before a raging storm and the beginning of a test that would challenge my faith. I walked slowly during the day. Co-workers made fun of me because I walked so slow. I wanted to scream and let them know that I was in pain. When I got home it was behind me and I didn't think too much about it. When I woke up the next morning my condition was the same and I had to press to get to work. This was the start of an unforeseen battle. My supervisor kept asking me if I'd gotten hurt at work. I replied, "No, I woke up like this." He also questioned the other employees. It got back to me that he was trying to replace me. It was no surprise to me that this was their intent. I realized I needed to find out what was going on before these people killed me. Yet with all that I was going through I still kept the faith, believing and trusting God—no matter what.

The weekend came, and I felt worse. On Monday, it was back to work again and I had to follow the same routine, pressing my way to work. My condition had worsened so much that I could no longer lift my right arm, because it was so heavy. I had to do job checks, which entailed a lot of copying documents.

It was hard for me to flip the pages when I was copying them. Answering the phone started to become very painful. I was so numb I couldn't feel it. If my hand had fallen off the counter or I dropped something out of my hand, I wouldn't have known because it was so numb. As I got worse and worse, I said to myself, *I can't do this any longer.* Here I was at a job, trying to pay my bills, knowing something was wrong with my health. I was worried about my job, and they weren't worried about me one bit.

My condition had changed my life completely. My daughter had to dress me, cook for me, and feed me most of the time. She did all of my errands and paperwork. I couldn't write at all. I felt so hopeless; I wanted to break down and cry. Something that comes out of nowhere and takes you by surprise can be a major blow; a blow that I really couldn't handle at that moment (and I didn't want to).

I kept thinking that maybe I was wrong about what I was feeling. I called on the Lord, saying, "King Jesus, I need you. I need to hear from you. I don't want anything negative in my spirit."

Finally on Wednesday, as I was on my way to work, I told my daughter that I needed to make an appointment to see our doctor. I was scared to death; I knew I had reached the point where it was now or never. I made an appointment for that Friday.

I could hardly make it into the doctor's office, because I was in so much pain. I was literally dragging my feet into her office. The pain was so severe, I wanted to drop and cry as if there was no tomorrow. With every step I took, as I felt the pain I called on the name of Jesus. This was between me and Jesus. As I'm writing this book, I can still feel the pain that I felt at that moment. I tell you, it was only by the Grace of God that I made it through that moment of my life. Nobody, and I mean nobody, but Jesus could have helped me or seen me through that trial.

I had just saw my doctor a couple weeks earlier, and she was amazed at the condition I was in. She ordered an emergency CT scan the same day and some blood work. After I was done I went home and I was thankful that they gave me the following week off because of my condition. After all that I had been through I needed a break at that point. During that week, my test results came back. My CT scan showed a little something in my neck. My blood test was normal, except for one thing, I was told that I was at the borderline for lupus. I really was shaken up, because my daughter's aunt had lupus, the pain she had suffered and the things she had gone through before she died was no joke. My doctor said I had to come back in six months to take another test to see if I was above or below the borderline. I thought, *Oh God, what is really going on?*

Then I got worse; now my twenty-year-old daughter had to help me to the bathroom. I couldn't even wipe myself, and that's bad. She bathed me, and had to help me in and out of bed. You name it she had to do it. It was wearing her out. I felt so bad but there was nothing I could do. I was so frustrated that I couldn't do it myself. I had to teach myself how to eat with my left hand, because my right hand was completely numb and of no use, and that was not easy at all. When my daughter fed me, I felt like an invalid. I couldn't walk straight, couldn't stand for three seconds. I've improved a little since then. Now I can stand at times for about five minutes. Praise God I've come this far! I have seen and heard of people going through similar or much worse than I. I was in awe when it happened to me. It made me think that I should never take life for granted.

When I went back to the doctor, she looked at me as if she couldn't figure out what was going on with me. Now I had a new issue that I had been dealing with. I told the doctor I had been itching on my right side, inside my body, 24/7. I itched from my neck to my foot, and across my back. I told her I couldn't scratch enough. I had scratch marks on the right side of my body. I had honestly started to think this was something like what Job had experienced in the bible. Wow, I could cry now just thinking about how bad the inside of my body was itching. It drove me nuts, much worse than the Chicken pox. The more I scratched, the more it itched.

I didn't know how to explain it, but my daughter understood because she was there and saw it firsthand. She said, "Ma, you're like Job in the Bible." Then she said, "Oh God, are we going to lose everything?" After she said that, I recalled that one of the things that happened to Job was that he lost his children and more. The moment she said that, the enemy started bringing things to my mind. I started to think we were going to lose everything. See, those spirits started making me think.

I said, "Lord, I got enough things I'm carrying. I cannot carry this load. This is enough to take me out of here." That is literally how I felt.

When I told my doctor about the itching, she asked me if I ever had Shingles. I asked her what that was. She explained that Shingles was a virus related to the Chicken pox virus, and then she asked if I had had the Chicken pox. I said yes. She said that I had Shingles, as soon as she said that my spirit dropped, the devil was on my trail. She gave me antibiotics for seven days. I did not miss a dose. I was so happy I had something for that itch that felt like I had fleas in and out of my body. Then my doctor told me she was sending me to a neurologist. I thought, *Lord this is deep, but it is not so deep that you can't handle*. By now with all the things that were happening to me my doctor and I knew that it was something seriously wrong with me.

Eventually, I had to go back to work, but I was not able to do my duties anymore. It was hard to use my arms and to walk and stand. When I went to the neurologist, he ordered two MRIs and some blood tests. When I had the first MRI, I thought I was going to choke in that machine. They tell you not to move, only breathe; plus they had to inject me with a needle. I was beside myself; my mind seemed to be in another place. I wanted to scream, *Let me out of here!* Finally, we were done. The next day I got a call telling me to come in for my second MRI. I panicked and told my daughter I didn't know if I could do it. But I knew I had to. My daughter went with me, and I could feel her hand rubbing my feet. Knowing she was there comforted me. I thought that if she wasn't there, those people would kill me.

One week later I got a call that my test results were in. I went to the doctor's office, and he explained that something was wrong with my nerves. I said that there were a lot of things going on with me. He told me he wanted me to get a spinal tap. I froze. I had heard about spinal taps and how you have to be still. You can't move at all. *This can't be happening*, I thought. He asked me if I was willing to do it. After several seconds I said yes, I would do it. I wanted to find out what was wrong, but not like this. The doctor thought I might have had a stroke, but that was not the case.

There are certain preparations you have to go through before you take a spinal tap. I had to take a lot of blood tests, and then I had to wait a week for the results. When the results came back, I got my appointment to take the spinal tap. Nervous, nervous, nervous! My nerves were shot.

Chapter 2

My Appointment

IT WAS ABOUT TWO weeks later after my last doctor's appointment the phone rang. When I saw the hospital's number, I knew why they were calling. Although I knew why they were calling I was calm when I answered the phone. The nurse was calling to give me the date for my appointment, and I said okay and hung up the phone. A couple of weeks before the appointment, the hospital called me several times, asking me the same questions. All their questions were making me very nervous. I told them my nerves would be wrecked completely before I had the test done. They asked me if I was sure I wanted to do this procedure. Did I know where I was supposed to go? Was I sure of the time? As I said, it was really nerve wracking.

For almost two weeks before the appointment, I woke up in the early hours of the morning. It was hard for me to go back to sleep, thinking about the procedure. The night before my appointment, I tried to stay calm, thinking and praying. Finally I went to sleep, and got up at 5:00 a.m. to get ready. I was nervous, but I knew God had everything under control. I arrived at the hospital at 7:30 a.m. and walked to the registration department to sign in. Then I had to go sign in with the nurse. About twenty minutes later, the nurse came to me and took me to an examining room to do vital signs, take blood, give me a shot, and ask me about a thousand questions. This all took forty-five minutes, and then the doctor came in to talk to me. He explained the procedure, including complications and symptoms. Finally, someone came to get me to take me to the procedure table.

As I slowly got on the table, I thought, *Oh God, I need you. Let everything go well.* Everyone else was moving quickly, and I silently said in my mind, *slow down.* I had to lie on my stomach. They put a sheet over my upper body and another one over my backside. The doctor came in and I couldn't move, it scared me to death. I wanted to cry. The doctor said he was going to wipe my lower back with some cold solution. I said okay. It was shivering cold, but I had to be still. Not only was the solution cold, the room was freezing. The doctor said he was going to stick me with a needle to numb me. I said okay. It hurt a little, and he then said he would be back to check if it was numb enough for the procedure. I said okay.

When the doctor came back to check, I thought, *Oh my God, he's going to stick me in my spine.* I wanted to scream to the depths of my soul. I wanted to jump off that table and run as fast as I could. I knew I had to be still and I tried to relax.

The doctor asked, "Do you feel that?"

Did I feel that? It hurt like there was no tomorrow. He was pressing on the numb spot so hard. My, my, my. Then it was over, and He said he'd be back in five minutes. I said okay. I waited, terrified as I talked to God. The Lord told me that everything would be all right.

The doctor came in, and I waited; waiting for him to tell me he was going to start the procedure. Before I knew it, I felt something going straight down my back in the numb area. I was so numb that I really couldn't tell if what I felt was the start of the procedure.

But as I lay there, the Holy Ghost let me know that he had already started the procedure. By that time the needle was halfway in… and we are not talking about a little needle. This was one of those jumbo needles that they use for these types of procedures. I was so still, I was way past good behavior, but then it was all over before I knew it. I had to sit up and be transferred to a gurney to go to the recovery room for two hours. My head hurt a little, but all I could think about was how awful the procedure was, how I wanted to scream, break down and cry.

I thanked and praised God for bringing me through that. In no time I was released to go home.

"Yes, Lord," I said.

I got home and my head started to hurt a little more. As the day passed my head hurt more. I couldn't eat or drink water. I tried to eat Jell-o, but that made my head hurt worse. I went to sleep, but when I woke up, boy, oh boy; my head was hurting so bad. This was one of the side effects of the spinal tap. When I moved in bed, my head would hurt. When I moved my foot or tried to get comfortable, my head would hurt. I tried to go to the bathroom, and I walked like a snail because every step was painful. I could hardly make it to the toilet. My daughter had to wipe me when I was done. I couldn't get up. It was so painful when I moved I had to sit still for twenty minutes to prepare myself to endure the pain that I felt every time I moved. I wanted to scream. All the time I was thinking, *Jesus help me. I need your help.* I was feeling ill and thought I was going to throw up. I tried to drink water, sipping it slowly, but that didn't work. My head felt like someone was banging on it and wouldn't stop.

Two days later, I woke up throwing up. My head still hurts. I cried, and sure enough, that made it hurt worse. I was already nervous from the pain, of not being able to walk, or to lift my legs, as well as losing my vision. I was torn up. I became frustrated, because I couldn't read the word of God. I asked someone to read to me, but they didn't want to. When they did read, it wasn't heartfelt. I asked the Lord why I was here. I struggled through life for this? My spirit began to grieve. I just wanted to hear the word of God. I began to talk to the Lord; the Lord began to talk back to me. He told me he had allowed this trial in my life to help make and mold me. I needed to see some things about me, my ministry, and people. Most of all God wanted me to learn more about him. So just imagine how I was feeling.

The fourth day, I wanted it to be over as quickly as possible. I tried to move around force myself to eat Jell-o or sip water. Although my body was in pain I managed to lie down but couldn't sleep because my head would hurt. When I did doze off, my head would pound as if someone had swung at me. I tried to sleep it off, most of that day. On days five and six, I began to eat a little, but I had to force the food down. Late at night on the sixth day the pain in my head began to lighten up. Day seven was better than day six. On the eighth day I was feeling a lot better, though the pain was still there. Day nine I began to eat more, even though I had to force myself. I started to feel sick again so I had to lie down. All this time I was waiting for my test results to come back. I just wanted to get better. When I stopped thinking about the test results, I received a call letting me know that the test results were in.

Chapter 3

Test Results

THE PHONE RANG. I answered, and the neurologist's receptionist said that my test results were back and the doctor needed to talk to me. My daughter and I went to see the neurologist, and I had my prayer warriors praying at the same time. I told myself to keep my mind on Jesus no matter what I heard. I thought about my cousin and the words she gave me from the Lord, and to listen to my mentor, a Mother in Zion.

We waited until they called me back to see the doctor. We sat down in his office and waited again until he came in. He had this look on his face and asked me who my primary doctor was. I knew God had given me a peace that I couldn't explain. It did not matter what the doctor said to me. It mattered what God said and the peace he had given me.

I took a breath, and the doctor said the test results showed I had Multiple Sclerosis. On the inside of me I felt the joy of the Lord. God was my strength. That was all I knew, and I had to apply what I knew. I was settled in my spirit and more calm than I had been at the beginning.

The doctor said I had a choice. I could take a shot seven days a week with an experimental drug. I said that was out, since I wouldn't know what they were putting in my body. The second choice was to take pills that hadn't been on the market long. Finally the doctor said that we could wait it out for three months to see what happened. He wanted to see if I had a relapse. During the 3 months he had me to stay home my daughter and I began to ask questions.

I knew this was the beginning, not the end. I learned it was not the test result that I needed to hear. I learned that it was Jesus I lived for. It was Jesus I would die for. He had every answer I wanted to hear. It's not what man says. It's about my Father which is in heaven. He decides what he wants me to hear. He decides if he wants me to wake up in the morning.

This joy that I have, the world didn't give it to me and the world can't take it away. I had to learn to turn my heart, mind, body, and soul over to Jesus.

God can do a miracle through a test result. Know that God is able. Keep your mind on the Lord. Stay focused and let go and let God take control. Yes, it was hard at first, but you learn that this is Jesus' business, not ours. God wants us to live life to the fullest. He wants us to abide in him. He will then abide in us and take care of the rest. Begin to build up your faith and trust God before you even take the test. Know that it's all right, no matter what the results are. Jesus has it all in control. Remember, he is our doctor. Our time may be almost up, but we should never give up, never stop pursuing the things God wants us to do. Never doubt who God is and what he can do. Run this race to the end.

Don't let a test result end your life. Instead, it should be the time when you keep pushing in the things of God. I once thought that test result would be the end for me, but the devil is a liar. That is the trick of the enemy. I had to fight, and I am still fighting on my good days and my bad days. Most of the time it is not easy for me, but I have to push running to Jesus, and my daughter makes me want to push. You still fight. Don't accept that test result in your spirit. Yes, it may be true what they say. So you begin to talk to God and pray to him.

You have to see what you need to do. One of the things I had to do was change my eating habits, exercise, and get massages on a regular basis. This helped, and it is still helping me. Some days I am not in a position to do everything I should, but when I can, I push and press. I keep my mind off me. I don't worry if I can't walk right or move my arms, or if I can pick my legs up, or if I can take a shower. All I can think of is the goodness of Jesus, how great he is, how wonderful he has been to me.

When I heard the test results, I wanted to shout, "Glory!" Why? Because my hope is in him. I felt the peace that God had placed within me. I said, "Lord, you know if I could do a hundred flips, I would." That's how happy I was. All I know is that someday I'm going home to meet my Father. That's what I think about. I'm not worried about people praying to see me down, now that they know what I'm going through. Really, if they only knew how happy I am! I pray for them, yes, Lord. Thank God for discernment.

Learn when you hear your results not to tell many people. Don't have so many people praying. Keep it to a select few. Why? You will find out not everyone who says they are there for you actually is. A lot of people are not praying for you they are preying on you. Don't listen to so many negative things that can get in your spirit and take you to another place, where you don't want to go. Then you find yourself depressed or going through troubles that are hard to get rid of. God will deal with you at this point if you allow him. Whatever God says, we have to learn to accept it.

Trust Jesus, not the test results.

Chapter 4

Multiple Sclerosis

THERE ARE DIFFERENT LEVELS of Multiple Sclerosis (MS). Some people are bedbound, blind, paralyzed, can't walk, can't eat, have problems breathing, numbness, aches and pains, and so on. Some may have all these symptoms, or only some symptoms.

Now that my illness has been diagnosed as multiple sclerosis I am learning how to deal with it every day. When it comes to walking, some days are better than others. Not being able to do for yourself is not something you expect to happen, but you know it could happen. My lifestyle has changed as I found myself unable to do the things that I used to do. I have to take it easier with the little things that in life are often taken for granted; like standing up. It is very difficult at times to get up because my legs give out from being tired. I find myself having to stay home a lot because of it.

It was really difficult to understand people who said they were there for me in this trying time of my life. Some knew my condition but I wouldn't hear from them. I couldn't understand when I sent out a text message to someone that was very important, to someone who I thought cared enough about me, I was wrong. The person texted me back three months later to answer the question I had asked them, "Is this for real?" I said to the Lord, and shook my head each time it happened. It was hard for me to understand. The Lord had to guide me through and teach me to concentrate; to lean and depend on him completely. Through this dilemma I was truly beginning to learn how to do just that.

Because of my condition, sometimes I felt like giving up, throwing in the towel. I said, "Why do I have to be here?" I was lied on, at my job people were plotting against me. I saw the enemy for what he was. I asked God to help me to let go of all the people who weren't there for me, who didn't mean me any good. Boy, oh boy, he did. I had no more tolerance for nonsense.

A prophetic word came to me. Someone said, "There are some people who are around you to drain you. I was surprised at some, because they claimed to be a Christian but their actions spoke against them. As for others I was not surprised." Then I was told, "It is what it is." I began to dwell on that word given by God, and as sure as I am sitting here writing, the Lord began to show me. Actually, all along he was trying to show me. Since I've been in this condition, he showed me how to love them from a distance. If they need prayer, I will pray for them. So far as going out together, that's not happening.

God began to show me in dreams the faces of people who said they were there for me but were not. *Wow, God,* I thought, *you are awesome.* I prayed with my mind on Christ, praying for them with a loving and forgiving heart. Then the Lord started to teach me about forgiveness. Ouch! It was hard not only to forgive some people who had hurt me, but those who were closest to me.

I couldn't comb my hair, but had to get it braided for four months. The last time, I had to take it out by myself because I was stubborn and wouldn't let anybody touch my hair. My hand was really paining me. I shouldn't have done it, but it had to be taken out. I said, "Lord, why am I here? Why?" The Lord said, "I'm making you."

I sat back and told the Lord that I understood. When you are down and can't do for yourself, praise God, struggling through every painful stroke trying to comb your hair or take a shower it's hard to see the brighter side. I began to have a change of attitude and my faith was elevated to another level and I began to speak life. I began to say "God you are able" "You are my healer. Make me whole, keep me safe. I want to do what you called me to do before I leave the earth. Wash me, cleanse me, and purge me." Still, every stroke of my hand was painful.

I began to say, "Lord, I thank you, I praise you, I magnify you, I lift up your holy name." I began to dig deep in the word of God. I needed the truth, I needed life in me. Day by day, slowly but surely, it didn't matter to me who was there for me or not. Jesus was my full concentration. I was about to lose my car, and couldn't even afford gas a lot of the times. I was getting ready to lose my apartment because I was no longer able to work. My situation could cause me to become homeless and unable to take public transportation because I couldn't walk one block or stand up for long. I couldn't go out for long periods of time, and people whom I know had the resources wouldn't help. I said, "Lord, when I die, let me die in the army of the Lord as a bold soldier, a bold warrior that fought the good fight of faith."

Regardless of what was going on, God was trying to reach me, teach me, and to grab my attention. He was trying to show me the distractions that got in my way. The Lord was showing me how to move by his spirit, how to pray in the spirit realm. *Wow wee, God, I prayed, I want more of you and less of me. Decrease me, Lord, and increase you.*

I began to feel the unction of the Holy Ghost to pray. God started showing me his mysteries and revelations in his word, through dreams and visions. I am able to see Jesus. I was so amazed by the beauty, kindness, and compassion in that light. So beautiful, I started to tap into God more and more, regardless of my condition.

I didn't worry about the MS hardly as much. I started eating healthy, exercising, not eating fried foods, and taking my herbs and vitamins. I began to feel an inner cleansing in my body. The enemy would try to attack, but I would say, "Satan, this body belongs to God."

Whatever your condition is, Jesus paid the price on the cross. The Lord had to dig deep down in me through my condition. I still don't feel good on some days, and my hands are still numb, but I am taking one day at a time.

Chapter 5

Having a Relapse

ONE DAY I WENT for a walk and my legs began to collapse. My bones and joints felt as if they could have snapped while I was walking. I was scared, that I might not make it back. I thought so many things, yet tried to concentrate on getting myself home. Everyone was looking at me but no one helped. Because I had over-walked myself my legs were moving as if I was crippled. *Devil, you are a liar*, I thought to myself. I wanted to burst out in tears, while trying to keep a sane mind by talking to the Lord. "Let me make it back, let me walk again." I prayed. I kept calling on the name of Jesus every step of the way, full of pain with each step I took.

My feet were hurting me so much and my legs were dragging. I was exhausted, and drained. I felt like I was about to drop. That's when I said, "Lord, with the breath I have in me I can make it." I began to rest in Him and I took my time walking slow, and taking rest stops in between. I just wanted to get into my bed and go to sleep. I didn't want to hear anything from anyone. I felt like I was having a breakdown, physically and mentally. Even though my daughter was walking next to me, there was not much she could do. I didn't want her to touch me. She said something to me, I was so frustrated I got mad at her and wanted no help. I didn't want to be bothered. I said to the Lord with a glimpse of hope as we got near our home. "Lord, we are just about there." I had to keep myself encouraged. I kept saying, "Come on, Jesus. Come on."

I felt embarrassed when I saw how the people kept looking at me. As we got closer to our home, I felt more relieved. I knew my daughter was nervous. She had never seen her mother this way. I apologized to her for how I'd reacted toward her. It wasn't a good feeling, not being able to get around and believing people have forgotten you. But Jesus Christ is the reason I'm here today. He is what keeps me going.

I had my second relapse in January 2011. I woke up feeling sharp pains in my left arm. It was making me feel a little nervous. The next day, I was feeling more pain. By the third day, when I moved my arm in a certain way, the pain made me want to scream. *Oh my, my, my,* I thought. *Satan, you can't have me,* I said in faith. You talk about a trial that was trying my faith; after I said it, both of my hands were now out of service. My right hand and wrist were still numb. I had to grab my left hand with my right hand, which was very hard. I would have to grab it to get up out of bed. If you ever had any encounters with this disease you understand how difficult it is to describe the pain. Really I can't. It was agony. I had to keep myself focus on calling on the name that was and is my help, Jesus!!!

I began to realize that God wanted me to get to the place of seeing that this sickness and pain was not my identity and it became my daily confession. As it says in John 10:10, *there is a thief who comes to kill, steal and destroy.* I will not let the return of any symptoms bring fear, but will resist them with the truth that God has healed me. It is especially beneficial for me to read the word of God daily and declare positive truths of myself, my home, and my finances, reaffirming it with thanksgiving. If you are going through any kind of illness or dilemma may you go forward in health and filled with hope, experiencing the grace of God, walking in your new identity, and overflowing with thankfulness.

Here are some scriptures that God has given me to share with you:

1 Peter 1: 23

Ephesians 1: 7

Colossians 1: 12

Hebrews 9: 14

1 John 1: 9, 2: 12

2 Corinthians 5: 17, 6: 19

Colossians 1: 13

1 Peter 1: 18-19

Galatians 3: 13

Chapter 6

A Call from My Physician

On February 14, 2011, I had to take my six month blood test to see if I was still on the borderline for Lupus. I was nervous; still my trust was in the hands of God. Later on that day, my cousin called me and said God had told her to tell me not to worry. "Everything will be all right. He's bringing you through every situation."

My spirit was a little low. I started to pray, because I didn't want to get too depressed or start feeling sorry for myself. I was sitting in the kitchen talking to the Lord, remembering what I studied earlier when I was reading the word of God. I went to lie down on the couch, trying to rest my mind. Suddenly the phone rang. It was my doctor. She said she needed to see me and I needed to make an appointment for the next day. I told her what I had told her assistant—I would go when I had enough money for the co-pay. The doctor asked me how much the co-pay was. I told her $25. She told me to make the appointment and she would waive the fee. She had never done that before, so I knew the results of my blood test were back. I was so nervous that it was causing my head to hurt.

My nerves were out of sorts, so I decided to keep busy. I got up and added this chapter to my book.

Finally I got up and went on my way to see my doctor. She told me my blood test had been positive for Lupus. I was at peace. I told myself that I'd already been through so much in my body. She explained that she didn't know if the test had come back positive because I have MS. It could be just the MS showing and not Lupus. She said she didn't want to put me on a new medication, because she didn't want the medications to clash and do damage to my body. So she recommended that I see a rheumatologist. I said "okay." God is the head of all of my decisions. Nobody could do me like Jesus; nobody could heal me like Jesus.

On February 24, I was getting ready to go to a revival when my leg started acting up. I couldn't walk straight. I had to hold onto the walls, and my breathing wasn't normal. I wanted to go to church; it saddened me because I couldn't. I went to lie down on the couch, and both of my arms started to ache. This was new, and this was a symptom I didn't want to feel. The pain got worse and I couldn't move my arms. I thought nervously, as well as I found myself beginning to understand, what my daughter's aunt had been saying when she suffered pain from Lupus. My hands began to harden. My right hand was painful and stiffer than normal. The fingers of my left hand ached. I kept still on the couch, praying that the pain would pass. My daughter had to help me into my bed, because I was in too much pain to make it to the bed myself.

I woke up the next day feeling as if I wanted to cry. I couldn't pray because my head, arms, and legs were bothering me so much. I tried to read and study the Bible, but I couldn't. My vision was blurry. I sat in my bed for several minutes, wondering to myself, "When would this end, and when will I be whole again?" I thought to myself, *I can't do this.* As I sat, I felt sharp pains in both my feet and toes. This was new. All I could do was pray, I prayed and prayed. I laid down, wanting to pray with someone but I laid there by myself, trying to pray for myself.

It was a difficult challenge for me to pray. Every time I prayed my head would hurt and my breathing would get short. As I waited for my daughter to wake up to bring me something to eat, my body was freezing cold and in much pain.

On the 26th day the pain had lessened, but my head hurt fiercely. I laid in bed all morning. Once I got up, I rested throughout the day, praying I would be better to go to church tomorrow.

The next day, I got up by faith on that Sunday morning, with the pain in my upper chest and my legs was acting up. I pressed my way to the service, eager to see the people who usually greeted the congregants at the door. That's what I look forward to when I go. There's warmth in that greeting. We walked in and no one greeted us or even acknowledged us. I sat down and raised my hand in praise and worship. When my hand got tired, I put it down. Pain crept through my right arm, into the fingers, wrist, and shoulder. My legs began to cramp, and I began to have pain in my upper chest. I just closed my eyes and I continued to worship God through the praise and worship. I couldn't move my arms, but my tears got their release. I heard the minister telling us to stand up and worship. I thought, *Lord, I can't stand up.*

No one knew my situation or what I was going through. If they had known, they would have reacted differently. I could hardly sit there and now I wanted to go home, yet I stayed. My soul needed the praise, worship, and word. After the service was over I went home. Even though people did not ask me how I was or if I was feeling all right, it was okay. I had Jesus on my side.

When I hear something pertaining to me, the enemy attacks my body. Using subtle cunning, he creeps up on me in my mind and thoughts, and then he works on my body. I know the devil can't have me. The devil is a liar. He has no truth in him. Praise God for Jesus. Trust, believe, and know that God is able, no matter how you feel, what you go through, or what happens in your life. Know Jesus will never leave nor forsake you (Heb 13: 5).

Chapter 7

Walk by Faith, Not by Sight

No matter what I'm going through, I have learned to walk by faith and not by sight. As I had to stay home on leave from my job because of my condition, I received a letter from my employer saying my disability leave had run out. I lost my job. I had been with the company for six years; the way they did it was so cold. The Lord had prepared me for this. Some of their hearts were so stone cold with the lies that were told about me and the way they spoke so nasty to me over the phone when I asked questions concerning the matter.

God had revealed to me the hearts of my supervisor and the human resource person I had to talk to. So losing my job didn't come as a surprise. But still, what was I going to do? I was the breadwinner of the house. I knew no one else would care and be there like I was for my household. I had to cancel a lot of things I had going on. I knew I couldn't keep them up with no finances. I looked at the situation, but I couldn't see it by faith. Bills were so overwhelming. Then God let me realize he had taken care of everything thus far. In that season of my life God started to show me how to really walk by faith, and not by sight.

As I began to rest in God, my faith became stronger and stronger. I had peace within. My condition would go up and down with the relapses, and I had to walk by faith. Dwelling on the situation didn't do me any good. Thinking what I could do or how I could fix it didn't help. But as I walked in faith, I was able to give it to God. God is my provider, he's my healer, he's King of kings and Lord of lords. He is Jehovah Rapha—the Lord will heal (Exodus 15: 26). He is Jehovah Jireh—the Lord will provide (Genesis 22: 13-14). He is Jehovah Shammah—the Lord is present (Ezekiel 48: 35). He is Jehovah Shalom—the Lord is peace (Judges 6:24). He is El Elyon—the most high God (Genesis 14: 17-20; Isaiah 14: 13-14). He is El Shaddai—God almighty (Genesis 17:1; Psalms 91: 1).

This is what I have to hold on to when I walk by faith. My faith has made me whole. I want to leave a legacy to my daughter to walk by faith, not by what she sees. My faith in God is how I came out of depression, oppression, being low and in a suicidal state of mind. God has allowed me to see he is doing this, not me or anyone else. When I found myself resting in God, I wasn't worried about people and how they reacted anymore. Yes, things would still blow my mind when it came to people who confessed to be saints but whose actions spoke differently. I would ask, "Where are the real saints?" I just couldn't believe how people were.

Chapter 8

Changing My Mindset

I HAD TO CHANGE my mindset and turn things completely over to God. Let's just say that God gave me a mind makeover. Everything around me had changed for the better. I was around a new set of people, a new atmosphere, with a new group of people at a new church. When God encouraged me to choose a new set of people to fellowship with it was one of the best things He has done for me.

It is very important to be around people who will tell you the truth. I was happy that a weight had been lifted off of me. I no longer had to worry about people not speaking to me in church and then talking to my daughter, not knowing they were really hurting her. Some, I'm sure, knew what they were doing. My mindset was in a new place now. Forgiveness had come in, as I talked about in chapter five. Every time something would happen, God would remind me of forgiveness, love, compassion, and understanding.

I no longer have to be afraid, angry, bitter, or walk in hatred. God has room for everyone. There are no more chains holding me down. I can fly now, and I'm going home to be with Jesus Christ. Wow, what an awesome God. Feels good, feels fresh. I think differently, and my actions are different. I am able to pray freely for someone else. Keeping our mind on Jesus is the best thing we can ever do. Ask God daily to help in situations that become hard for you. Begin to plant the word of God in your heart and mind. When we do this I found out there is no room for us to concentrate on anything else.

Chapter 9

It Could Happen to You

NEVER DOUBT THAT AS you live from day to day something could happen in your life that would change your life forever. Know that what happened to me could happen to you. We don't know from one day to the next what will change in our lives. We can't alter the plan and purpose that God has laid out for us. I read Paul's writings in the Bible, and I can imagine when he was converted into Christianity, he had no idea of the suffering that came with it. I could imagine him saying that it wasn't what he signed up for.

When we suffer for Jesus it may seem unbearable, just keep this in mind, God will not put more on us than we can bear (2 Corinthians 1: 8-10). His grace is sufficient. It doesn't matter what form, shape, size, or color we are, no one is exempt. Will you stop praying to God if a sickness or disability comes upon you, or a loved one, or even an enemy? What would you do?

Do you hold a certain position and think nothing will happen? Think again! Do you laugh at others? Do you ignore someone who has become sick and is bedbound? Is it someone that you may know who can't leave his or her house, shop for themselves, or even drive like he or she used to? Have you stopped calling that person, because you feel he is less than you? Or do you find yourself too busy? Just remember, *it can happen to you.*

I pray that my story has provoked something deep down inside the hearts of everyone that will cause them to think about taking someone in need some groceries or putting money in their hand. Maybe you can volunteer to do their hair, wash clothes, or clean their house. Most importantly, you can pray with them and let them know it will be all right, that God loves them. You can read the word of God to them as well.

Chapter 10

A Heart Filled with Compassion

BEING IN THE FIRE of this trial has brought me a little closer to becoming as pure as refiners gold. In the fire I've learned how to have a heart of compassion for others by going through my own trials. This condition changed my life. It allowed the pit of my soul to become transparent. I was able to see depression and oppression as well as I could see the pain, hurt, and wounds. I asked. "God is this how people are?" Where was the compassion?

Deep down inside, the pain was so severe that it was causing the pain I was feeling in my head day after day. I know now that it was the very thing causing depression. It made me feel as if there was a tractor trailer on me and it would not move. The weight of it held me down spiritually, mentally, and physically. I cried. "Jesus, Jesus, Jesus, I need your help."

I asked the Lord where the compassion of his people was. The Lord began to give me understanding. One of the things he began to show me was that people were jealous. It has moved me to ask for more and more compassion for all people. Now I pray for others with a greater compassion, whether it's someone close, or an associate, or an enemy. It doesn't matter. Even now I find myself praying for them.

As I prayed, God allowed me to feel their hurt, sadness, and wounds. It made me feel like I never want anyone to suffer any kind of sickness hurt, pain or disease. I asked the Lord to show me what I could do to help others. I might not be able to walk at times, or move my hands, but I have been able to encourage several people in situations and conditions similar to my own. This is the compassion that God has allowed me to develop in all that I have gone through.

Chapter 11

The New Me

I UNDERSTAND NOW WHAT it is to walk in the newness of Jesus Christ found in (Romans 6: 4). A new change began to take place. From a new set of clothes, a new hairdo, a new walk with integrity, and a new woman of God who has learned how and who is still learning to wait on God. This trial has caused my faith to grow in believing in the promises of God in his word. I know who God is, and I don't worry about anything. I am quiet, and I remain humble, as I meditate on the word of God. I get up in the early morning, between the hours of one and six starting with a new bible study in God's word. I receive new revelations and mysteries in His word that He has shown me, that weren't birthed out of my mind's imagination. My eyes were opened and my heart was opened and I was growing more sensitive to the things of God. Nothing else mattered. All I could say was, "God, have your way and let your perfect will be done." I tell you I felt brand new, and still do. God taught me how to have faith on this journey I am now traveling. This is what God was trying to show me all along. With my life in his hands, I no longer look at my condition of Multiple Sclerosis or my circumstances.

I now find myself looking to the hills from which cometh my help (Psalms 121: 1), I know that God is supplying all of my and my daughter's needs (Philippians 4: 19). As I wake up each morning I talk to the Lord. I tell Him that I want more of him and less of me. Even when I had more relapses and I would feel up one day and down the next. There were days when I couldn't walk or stand up for long periods of time.

God taught me how to depend on him and not worry. I didn't worry about anything any longer. I didn't worry about what the doctor said or what could happen. God told me he was in control. As sure as I am writing this book, I knew in my spirit that God had everything in his hands. I had a peace that was out of this world, and I knew no one could have given me that peace but God. With this kind of thinking I felt things lifting off me. Regardless of how I felt, I knew I had to praise my way through it all. God taught me about praising him. I praised God. I worshipped God. When the attacks came, with my body filled with pain, God showed me how to recognize the enemy. I didn't and don't have time to walk around depressed or concentrating on me or other people. I didn't have room for anything negative, only to walk in my calling. That's where my mind is, and I love it. Praise God, I just want to be ready when Jesus comes.

Chapter 12

Covered by the Blood of Jesus Christ

I'VE COME TO REALIZE that I am covered by the blood of Jesus. Being born again, I know that the blood of Jesus that was shed for us covers me. I have learned over the years to plead the blood over my ministry, myself, my family, home, finances, etc. I am a child of God and I am covered by Jesus' blood. I am happy to be free and know that Jesus has me covered. He's not like us, what he gives he doesn't take back as many of us would do. The blood of Jesus is the foundation of our redemption. When Christ died our protection was connected with the shedding of his blood. There is power in the blood. This is something no man could have given or done for us.

How do we feed from the body of Jesus? *"And Jesus said to them, I am the bread of life; he that cometh to me shall never hunger; and he that believeth on me shall never thirst."* (John 6: 35). We feed on Jesus by coming to him and believing in him. Coming to him means having a heart that is drawn toward Jesus. We are to seek God with all our heart, mind, and strength. We receive from God by faith. Those who believe in him receive his blood and all its benefits. At the cross, Jesus' body became our bread and his blood became our drink. When we feel weak and hungry, we must return to the cross. There we will find nourishment, strength, and satisfaction.

Jesus taught his disciples to remember his sacrifice for them.

> *And he took bread, and gave thanks, and broke it, and gave unto them, saying, this is my body which is given for you: this do in remembrance of me. Likewise also took the cup after supper, saying, this cup is the New Testament in my blood, which is shed for you. (Luke 22: 19-20)*

We are to partake of communion to remember his broken body and the blood that he shed for us. By remembering the cross, we come to him, and by faith we receive him. Now that we are partakers of the blood of Jesus, the Holy Spirit empowers us to give our lives to God and serve him in the spirit of holiness.

When we remember the cross of Christ and receive his broken body and blood, we partake of the power of God. For the message of the cross is foolishness to those who are perishing, but to us who are being saved, it is the power of God (1 Corinthians 1: 18). We are being saved continually from things that attack us physically, mentally, and spiritually; things that threaten to distract us from serving our God in holiness. Where do we find relief, protection, and more power? The answer is, at the cross.

We overcome by the blood of the Lamb, Jesus Christ, and the word of our testimony. Through the blood of Jesus and our witness of it, we overcome and have power to give our life fully for the one who gave his life for us. We apply the blood by the word of our testimony. In the old covenant, they applied the blood by sprinkling it (Hebrews 9: 19). In the new covenant, we apply the blood by our words.

Every Christian's testimony has the same beginning. It begins on the cross of Jesus Christ. The blood that Jesus shed is the most important part of any testimony. Without the blood, we have no testimony. At the cross our testimony began, at the cross we were transformed, at the cross we were crucified with Jesus. I have been crucified with Christ. It is no longer I who live, but Christ lives in me. The life which I now live in the flesh I live by faith in the Son of God, who loved me and gave himself for me (Galatians 2: 20).

When we apply the blood of Jesus, Satan cannot touch us. You can apply the blood of Jesus to your body to receive healing (Isaiah 53: 5). You can apply the blood of Jesus to your mind to receive a sound mind. You can apply the blood of Jesus to your home (Exodus 12: 13). You can apply the blood of Jesus to your children's lives (Job 1: 5). You can apply the blood of Jesus to anyone and anything that you have authority over or influence upon. It is your right as a child of God. Also, in obedience to God's Holy Spirit you should apply the blood of Jesus to anything or anyone that he tells you to; it is your duty as a royal priest of the most high God. But you are a chosen generation, a royal priesthood, a holy nation, his own special people, that you may proclaim the praises of him who called you out of darkness into his marvelous light (1 Peter 2: 9).

I'm covered by his blood.

Chapter 13

My Friend Had a Dream

IN JANUARY 2010, I received a letter from a friend of mine. In the letter she wrote about a dream she had had, in which I got sick and died. She was worried about me. As I read it, it started to bother me; and each day the words burrowed deeper into my spirit. I thought I was really going to die. I started to question God, and then depression kicked in.

When I got sick in August 2010 I remembered the dream that my friend had; then I thought; I am going to die. I started to be fearful of death then all of a sudden I could hear my cousin's words, "Gee, speak life." That's what I began to do and I could feel life come in me more and more each day.

I called my cousin and talked to her about it. She told me the enemy wanted to deposit death in my spirit. She said, "Gee, *speak life*. Read certain scriptures." She told me to speak positive things into my life. She prayed with me and said we were going to fight together in prayer. Still, some days the thought would come back.

I would study and pray, and God showed me that when he says it's over, it's over. I said, "Praise God." God said, "Continue to walk in me."

Keep your eyes on me. Keep your ears open to hear my voice. He let me know that the enemy comes to steal, kill and destroy (John 10: 10). The enemy will come to take away everything that he can.

There are times when people will have a prophetic word to tell you. This wasn't the case for me. Know the word of God for yourself. Don't get caught without knowing the word. Then if we hear anything, we know it's coming from the Lord. I thank God I didn't let my friend's dream get me to the point where I began to embrace the thought. The enemy tries to plant words in our hearts. Fight back with your sword, which is the word of God. Learn how to seek God, learn how to wait on God. Don't accept the first thing you hear. Always take it to God in prayer. We don't want to become bitter or believe a lie in our hearts.

Sometimes a true word will come forth. Know your Bible and take heed of the things of God. Do not let things people say depress, bother, confuse, or sidetrack you. Push through what you hear, whether negative or positive. Know who you believe in, and that God has the first and the last say. God is the author and finisher of our faith. He is alpha and omega. He sits high and looks low; there is nobody greater than God. God is our peace. We are to learn how to walk in the peace that God has given us. We are the door keepers of our minds and hearts. Keeping our minds on God will keep our minds at ease when we hear something that is contrary to his word. In this is the comfort of God. Let go and let God do what he has to do in our lives.

Trust and stand on God's word.

Chapter 14

Know That You're Blessed

ONE THING I WANT every believer to know for sure is that when we're going through the storms, whether it is good or bad, we are blessed. There will be problems, circumstances, sicknesses, diseases, that will come. When we're going through we must say to ourselves, Didn't God wake me up this morning? Don't I have breath in my body? It is a blessing to see another day. Someone did not wake up this morning. We are blessed to have the breath that God has given us. God decided to keep us alive. *We are blessed, blessed, blessed.*

My heart is with God and my life belongs to him. I am forever his. My confession is that I am blessed. God loves us unconditionally. He does not love us one day and the next day his mind is changed. He will never fail us; he knows what's best for us. He knows how to catch our attention. God doesn't change. We are blessed for he is the same yesterday, and today, and forever (Hebrews 13: 8).

Jesus died for us when he didn't have to. He was beaten for us. They hung him high, pierced his side, put nails in his hands. Blessed is the one who loves God. Blessed is the one who praises God and walks in God's ways. (Psalms 103: 2) says, *"Bless the Lord, O my soul."* We are blessed when we can speak of God's goodness. He has supplied our every need. When we have clothes on our back, food to eat, a roof over our heads we are blessed. What person can give that to us? No one! God got it all for us. You are still here. There is a song that says I am still here.

Praise God, and to him be all the Glory, we are blessed. Can't nobody do us like Jesus. No one can fill you with the power of the Holy Ghost but God himself. Only God can fix our troubles. God won't leave us hanging. He will not act funny with us. He will not talk about us. He will not stab us in the back. God will not leave us alone. He won't hurt us. He cares about us. He watches over us. He protects us from all harm, hurt, and danger, seen and unseen. He covers our families with his blood. He is our refuge. He is our shepherd. He is our bright and morning star. He is our judge. He is our lawyer in the courtroom. He is our doctor. He is our deliverer. He is our strength. He is our redeemer. He is our shield. He is our counselor. He is our creator. He is all-knowing. He is eternal. He is love. He searches the heart. He gives unspeakable joy. The list goes on and on.

We are blessed. No one can be everywhere at the same time. No one can know everything, but God knows everything all the time. No one has all power, but God does. And he loves us.

We are so blessed to have someone, and not just someone, but God Almighty, who is concerned about us. It matters to God if we live right and accept Jesus as our Lord and Savior. He wants us to be happy and to see us walk in our destiny. We are blessed, blessed, blessed. Don't forget who comes first in our lives, and that's Jesus Christ.

He died for us. We are blessed.

Chapter 15

Persevere

We have to learn how to persevere, when we are going through whatever comes against us. We have to know and understand that God is there with us at all times. He wants us to press through, no matter how we feel. He wants us to stay focused on him and give life everything we have. Facing your conditions, circumstances, trials, etc., you have to know that this is not the end. You have to know that what you're going through it is not your destiny. We have to move forward in faith, believing and trusting in God.

Many times we don't know why things happen, but God does. I learned how to deal with my condition. No matter how hard it got, I had to push through. No matter how people treated me I had to realize it was not about me. By staying focused, it helped me to get to the next level to see what God has for me. It has been rough, and there were times I wanted just to say to the Lord, "This is enough." I even thought about ending my life.

Two things kept me going. No matter how hard it got for me, the two that kept me strong and fighting to live was Jesus and my daughter. I had to keep my mind stayed on Jesus; I knew he was the only way and life for me. The thought would come to my mind about going to hell if I took my own life. That was not a place I wanted to be so I kept on pressing forward, keeping heaven in my view. Heaven was where I wanted to be and heaven was my home. My daughter was my second encouragement. She was in my thoughts on those rough days when it was really difficult to deal with the pain. I would say to God, "There's more to you, Lord. There's more for me to know, to see, to experience."

I just couldn't see myself giving up. I learned how to keep pressing by keeping my mind on the word of God. As I walked with God, it made me want to be closer and closer to him. I knew it was not about me or other people. I was so worried at this point, about having a personal relationship with Jesus.

In your journey through tough times, you will hear a lot of negative things. You have to make up your mind not to listen to, or be around, those types of people. When negative energy comes at you, press on and speak the things of God. That's the only way you are going to make it. Know how the enemy is working against you to try to destroy you. Then fight back with what God has given you. No matter what your doctor says or how much people tell you that you're not going to make it, press and know who your healer is. Know that people don't have a heaven or hell to put you in, but God does. Keep pushing forward. Keep pressing. You are fighting for your very soul. So if in your struggle you have to let some people, places, and things go, then so be it. Do what you have to do.

Hardships will come, continue to press on in God. It doesn't matter what sickness, disease, hurt, or pain afflicts us. Press toward the mark (Philippians 3: 14). Let all the Glory be to God, and know that we have the victory. Think and speak on the things of God. Let nothing stop you; even if you can't get out of bed, can't move, can't talk, and can't walk, whether it was your fault or not. Keep speaking positively to yourself, whatever your condition is. Get scriptures to read pertaining to your situation. Put some encouraging scriptures on the walls around you. Play it on your earphones at night while you're sleeping. If it is a sickness or disease, get some healing scriptures Read the scriptures daily.

We have to learn how to press through depression, self-pity, etc. Know it is not of God to feel this way. It is of the enemy so he can take our soul, and keep our minds off of God. This is how the enemy tricks us. He wants us to give up, to think we have nothing to live for. *The devil is a liar.* He has already been defeated. Press through the lies of the enemy. Jesus paid the price for us on the cross which gives us the strength and the reason to press. We have to walk in that knowledge and let God take control.

When we don't press onward, we are showing the devil that he has us and it is telling God that we don't believe in him. If you believe that he is God but your faith is growing weak for your healing, just say I believe Lord please help my unbelief. God will meet you at the level of your faith. Don't let the enemy take control of your mind. He doesn't care about you or me. He's not concerned about how you feel. But he is concerned about how he can steal everything we have in and with God. He's concerned about how he can destroy us, and he is concerned about killing us and everyone we know. He wants our life and he won't stop until he has it. This is why we need to press through it all. God said, *"No weapon that is formed against thee shall prosper."* (Isaiah 54: 17). This is his word. Believe it, speak it, and know it.

Perseverance can be difficult, looking at the things that happen. We all have to go through something in our lives. God said he will not put more on us than we can bear (1 Corinthians 10: 13).

Chapter 16

One Year Later

I REMEMBER IT AS if it were yesterday. This trial came into my life and took me by storm. I bonded with Marvin Sapp, "Never would have made it [without you]"; so much more after this experience. This is what I can say one year later. I wouldn't have made it if it wasn't for the Lord who was on my side. Thank you, Lord. You saved me from harm, hurt, and danger. God gave me these scriptures to sustain me in the time of my adversity:

1 Samuel 15: 22, Psalms 1, Psalms 23, Psalms 27, Psalms 37, Psalms 91, Psalms 119, Proverbs 3: 5-6, Isaiah 26: 3, Isaiah 53: 5, Isaiah 54: 17, Isaiah 59: 19, Matthew 16: 18, Mark 5: 36, Mark 11: 23, Luke 10: 19, John 3: 16, John 10: 3-5, Romans 8: 11-13, Romans 8: 31, Romans 14: 23, Galatians 3: 13, Hebrews 3: 1, Hebrews 12: 2, James 1: 22, 1 Peter 2: 24, 3 John 1: 2, Revelation 12: 11. I meditate and go over each of them every day.

God allowed me to see that I could make it with him, the one who cares about me. He wanted me to see that my end is not based on a doctor's report. God told me to trust, believe and have confidence in him. My mind is changed. This experience has become an enlightening one. It has brought me a deeper level of understanding and revelation in his word. I saw how I will be able to help someone else, with all that he has given me to encourage myself. This trial has already opened doors for me to do ministry.

God put in my spirit the scripture that says to think on things that are lovely. I would get excited, because I recognized instantly what he had done. The joy in my spirit would cause me to be eager to go straight into his word. When I turned to Philippians 4: 8, I was happy because I knew God didn't want me to wallow in what the devil had for me. See, the enemy wanted me to sob in depression. I would resist and say, "No devil. Get off me. You can't have me. I'm God's property." Then I would turn to the scripture and read:

> *Finally, brethren, whatsoever things are true, whatsoever things are honest, whatsoever things are just, whatsoever things are pure, whatsoever things are lovely, whatsoever things are of good report, if there be any virtue, and if there be any praise, think on these things. (Philippians 4:8)*

That was the whole truth and nothing but the truth from God. What more could I ask for from the bible other than that one scripture? That gave me ammunition to stomp on the devil's head even more. I began to fight back with the word, praying to have my armor on, ready for battle. This was when I didn't worry about my condition. Why? Because Jesus and I are one! He already paid the price. It is done and settled in heaven. I have the victory. Satan is defeated.

I began to say, "I see myself healed, I see myself delivered, I see myself set free." I still say that over and over again. I'm healed in the name of Jesus. I believe it, I see it, and I know it. I keep letting that get in my spirit so it can dwell in my mind and heart. The words are planted on the inside, and the outside they become beatified in the glory of God. I'm thankful and give God the entire honor. I belong to him, I am not my own. God has done some amazing things within this year, whether I was willing to accept it or not. Lord, I thank you for who you are. The year has gone by so fast.

One year has passed with me in my current condition. There have been some ups and some downs. I have been going forward as a soldier without turning back. One of the things I am learning is, like Paul said, I am pressing toward the mark. Through the pain in my body, when I can't walk, I'm still pressing onward. Keeping myself busy doing the things of God makes me happy. By not concentrating on myself, I have learned to concentrate on God, to know who he is and what he can do.

There were times when I knew in my mind and felt in my body that it was time to go, but God said no. Barely holding on, unable to pick my legs up and walk in a straight line, pain in my body from head to toe, my vision blurry, there was nothing I could do but pray.

Some days it felt like I was walking on exposed bone, as if I had no skin. But God showed me how to move in him, without doubt. No matter how hard it has been, I have kept moving. If I hadn't, I wouldn't be here to finish this book. I have lived thus far to tell my story. When any man said I wouldn't or couldn't make it, God said I could. I don't take life for granted. I know what God has done and is doing. Whenever I thought it was over, God said it wasn't over. When I thought there was no way, he said he would make a way. When I said I couldn't see my way through, God said he could see. I just had to believe. He rewards those who diligently seek him.

God showed me how to praise him through every difficult circumstance and every tough situation. He taught me how to keep my eyes on him. He showed me how to put my confidence in him, not man. No matter what situation arose in my life, God helped me; and the situation allowed me to mature. It has been painful, completely shutting the world out when I knew I hadn't lied, hadn't done anything wrong, I had to trust God and encourage myself by reading, fasting, praying, and trusting in him.

My cousin always helped me and encouraged me. I am most grateful to God for allowing her to be my family and to take the time to help me through my low times.

For me, being in the low times feels like being dropped off in the wilderness with no way out. It feels like a dry, dry desert where I have been left to die. A storm would rise, but it wouldn't overtake me. God shows me how to have peace within. How I can have life and live more abundantly. I might be in that storm, but a wind comes that picks me up and turns my situation around. God said, whatsoever things are true, honest, lovely, and of a good report give him praise. In other words, he was saying to me he is truth. His word is true. Nothing about him is false, and he is with me. He will provide. To this day, God has provided when I thought it was over. Only God could have done this. He makes a way for me right on time. He showed me how to build my faith, war in the spirit, wait on him, hear his voice, and believe in him.

What an awesome, awesome God. My heart belongs to Jesus. I wouldn't change. There's nobody greater than God. He is my healer, my provider, my strength, my refuge, my shield, my rock. I can go on about how good God is.

One year later, I am walking better than I was. God connected me with a sister that had suffered with MS, who told me her testimony about some immune system pills and other products that help her. She was bound in a wheelchair for years. Today she's walking and everything. I began taking those same immune system pills and it has helped me tremendously. I am able to lift my right hand even though it remains numb and can be very painful with too much use. I thank God for every moment. Some days I'm amazed at what

God has done and is doing with me in this condition. This past year has been an unforgettable journey. I pray that all that I have gone through brings healing and becomes a blessing to all who read this book. I should have been dead or paralyzed, look at God! The last thing I would like to leave you with is I am still here without being paralyzed or dead one year later!

Chapter 17

What Is Multiple Sclerosis?

IF I WAS GOING to fight a good fight I had to learn and come to understand what multiple sclerosis was. Multiple Sclerosis is an inflammatory disease of the Central Nervous System that affects the brain and spinal cord. It causes a loss of control with the muscle, vision, balance, and sensation in the way of numbness. Multiple sclerosis causes damage to the nerves of the brain and spinal cord by the immune system. This is called autoimmune disease.

Autoimmune disease is when one's immune system normally goes out and destroys bacteria; it begins to, without knowing, attack normal tissue. In those that have MS, the immune system attacks the brain and the spinal cord. It attacks the nervous system. Other autoimmune diseases are Lupus and Rheumatoid Arthritis.

Our central nervous system is made up of nerves that act as the messenger of our bodies. These nerves are covered with a fatty substance called Myelin, which insulates the nerves impulses or messages, between the brain as well as the other body parts. These messages control muscle movements like walking and talking.

Sclerosis is the buildup of scar tissue in the brain and/or in the spinal cord. This is also were MS gets its name from.

The scar tissue comes when Myelin, the part that covers, protects and insulates the nerves, is destroyed. This process is called demyelination. If the Myelin's electrical signals don't go throughout, the brain the spinal cord is disrupted causing it to come to a halt. When this happens the brain is unable to send and receive messages. This breakdown is what causes the symptoms of MS.

Myelin in the body can be restored; unfortunately the process is not fast enough to outpace the deterioration that occurs in MS. The types of symptoms and how severe it can be and the course of MS varies widely. It is partly due to where the scarred tissue is located and the extent of demyelination.

According to the National Multiple Sclerosis Society, approximately 400,000 Americans have MS. It is also, with the exceptions of trauma, the most frequent cause of neurological disability which starts in early to middle adulthood.

MS is said to be more common in females than males. It is said to be two to three times as common. It is unusual to occur before adolescence. The risk of teens getting the disease is increased up to the age of 50. The risk begins to decline after.

The most common early symptoms of MS include:

Tingling numbness, loss of balance, weakness in one or more limbs, blurred or double vision.

These are said to be the less common symptoms of MS, slurred speech, sudden paralysis, lack of coordination, cognitive difficulties.

As it progresses, other symptoms may include muscle spasms, sensitivity to heat, fatigue, changes in thinking or perception, and sexual disturbances.

Fatigue is a common symptom of MS. It may consist of increased muscle weakness, mental fatigue, sleepiness, or drowsiness.

Muscle spasms are common with MS. It usually affects the muscles of the legs and arms, and may interfere with a person's ability to move those muscles freely.

Dizziness off balance or lightheaded these symptoms are caused by damage in the nerve pathways that coordinate vision and other inputs into the brain that are needed to maintain balance.

Impaired thinking; this means slowed thinking, decreased concentration, or decreased memory.

Vision problems can result in blurring or graying of vision or blindness in one eye. However, most vision problems in MS do not lead to blindness.

Abnormal sensations such as "pins and needles," numbness, itching, burning, stabbing, or tearing pains.

Speech and swallowing problems; with MS people often have swallowing difficulties. They are associated with speech problems as well caused by damaged nerves.

Tremors can be difficult to treat.

Difficulty walking is the most common symptom of MS. Muscle weakness and/or spasticity, numbness in your feet.

Other symptoms include breathing difficulties, bladder and/or bowel problems and seizures.

Everyone is different and should follow the instructions that you are given. What works for me may not work for you.

Chapter 18

How to Eat

IT IS SAID THAT change isn't easy. Often when a drastic change occurs it is ushered in by some unexpected dilemma leaving us no choice but to change. My eating habits were about to encounter a metamorphic change. I had to learn what I could or could not eat.

The things I couldn't eat included meat products, dairy products, including cheese and milk, with the exception of small amounts of fat free milk products. I learned that cheese and milk are considered beef products for those with MS. Processed foods should be eliminated, along with white sugar. I also learned that Multiple Sclerosis can be helped by changing the way I eat. It was said that fresh fruits and vegetables would reduce inflammation and lessen the pain. I learned that raw vegetables are best to eat for people with Multiple Sclerosis.

I learned that there are fats that are recommended to help those with Multiple Sclerosis. These fats are Omega 3, Omega 6, or from foods that have these in them or in supplement form. Vitamin D is very much needed. This can also be taken in pill form if you are not getting enough from foods. It is important to ask your doctor for a list of recommended supplements. It was said that many people that have been diagnosed with Multiple Sclerosis have become vegetarians.

Words of Encouragement

Trust God
Never give up
Believe in you
You can make it
You are somebody
Greatness is in you
Keep your head up
Learn to walk by faith
Encourage yourself daily
Quitting is not an option
Put God before all things
Stay focused and go forward
Press through your condition
Decide you will break through
Know that you are not forgotten
Have no doubt the impossible will happen
Keep in mind; the battle is not yours it's God's

Coming Soon

New Book Release

By Georgette Mayberry

Speaking Engagements

If you would like Georgette Mayberry to come to your ministry, events, book signings, etc., you can contact her at:

Email: evangelistgee@yahoo.com

Facebook: @GeorgetteMayberry

Twitter: @EncouragerGee

Website: www.georgettemayberry.com

It

Could

Happen

To

You

PHOTO CREDIT

Brigitte Coston

www.ingramcontent.com/pod-product-compliance
Lightning Source LLC
Chambersburg PA
CBHW020618130526
44591CB00042B/238